THE KEY POINTS!

THE KEY POINTS!

The Book of GENESIS and
The Book of EXODUS

Faye Ivey-Jones

author-HOUSE®

AuthorHouse™
1663 Liberty Drive
Bloomington, IN 47403
www.authorhouse.com
Phone: 1-800-839-8640

Published by AuthorHouse   08/08/2012

ISBN: 978-1-4772-5555-1 (sc)
ISBN: 978-1-4772-5670-1 (e)

Library of Congress Control Number: 2012914052

"The Key Point of "The Key Points!"

Through the inspiration of the Holy Spirit, I have adapted and written *"The Key Points!"* which is scripturally based on "The Message Bible", written by Eugene H. Peterson. The sole purpose for this writing of the Christian Doctrine of the King James Version translation, is an attempt to **simplify the bible stories contained within its pages to appeal to those readers who desire to learn of its contents but find the in-depth and repetitive text too overwhelming.** It is <u>not</u> in any way intended to disrespect, down play, minimize or replace any part of the "Holy Scriptures" as they have been recorded by the original translators. *"The Key Points!"* is a condensed summary of each chapter identified by chapter number for quick and easy reference to the actual original bible translation, followed by a list of questions that are relevant to each chapter. To further enhance the reader's knowledge and encouragement to become more familiar with God's Word, several questions have been derived that can only be answered by reading the original bible translational text.

My sincere hope is that this simplified, condensed writing of *"The Key Points!"* in part, for you readers who consider yourselves "Unlearned Christians". serve as a catalyst to accelerate change and awaken a healthier awareness of life, as seen through the eyes of God with you in it! It is my belief that upon reading these key points, you will become intrigued enough by its summaries to progress to a heightened level of curiosity and become hungry to want to know more about communing with our God who is within you. By studying the original translations, you will develop a broader insight on what you could avail yourself to by knowing and understanding the essence of your blessing and experience God's purpose, plan and promise for your life. Without a doubt, this will be gained by comparing how the blessing worked in the life of those who walked with God, opposed to the consequences of those who did not . . . . (selah)

The **BIBLE** is a spiritual, detailed roadmap inspired by God that guides us through the **B**asic **I**nstructions **B**efore **L**eaving **E**arth, and undoubtedly enhances the lives of all who journey through its pages. The good news is, God really loves us and wants to bless us!! Reading "**The BIBLE**" helps us to understand how to receive our blessing! So get started. Learn how to take hold of your blessing by reading God's Word.

I thank God for His tender mercies that come upon me that I may live; His law is my delight! (Psalm 119:77 KJV) Therefore, if any man be in Christ, he is a new creature, old things are passed away: behold all things become new! (2Corinthians 5:17 KJV)

Be Blessed!! Receive the Message of God's Word and Walk Therein!!

Joyful Lady Faye Ivey-Jones, Author
"The Key Points!"
<u>ProMovement@aol.com</u>   Read the Bible along with *"The Key Points!"* series

Thank You Father God,
For Your Tender Mercies, for Your Love and Inspiration, and Your Wisdom and Grace in the writing of this Labor of Love. As this work is viewed by each reader, may You Be Glorified and Your Will Be Done on Earth as it is in Heaven! In Jesus' Name . . . . Amen!

To My Brothers and Sisters in Christ,

* Sister Elaine Petry *	*** Apostle Erwin Lee Trollinger Jr. ***
* Minister Brenda Gilliam *	*** Ministers George & Danielle Peters ***

I thank God for you! With deep appreciation, I dedicate this series to you for pouring into my life and sharing your insight and Godly counsel by speaking and being "Doers" of the Word. You continually and freely give me encouragement and support as you do everyone you come in contact with. Thank you for your input to this project and for allowing God to use you as you answered the Call and progressively sow the seed of God's Word in your heart, thereby manifesting His Presence as **"Living Epistles"** for all the world to witness!

Everlasting Love & Gratitude,
Faye

I Thank God for blessing me with His gift of my family:
My Loving Parents Homer & Gladys Ivey, My Late Husband Danny Mitchell Jones

My Amazing Children & Grandchildren

Kyle Ramar Ivey-Jones, Kyron Danny Ivey-Jones, Tashi Ayala Ivey-Jones, Teresa Pina Ivey-Jones, Kytresa Faye Ivey-Jones, Kyanna Marie Ivey-Jones, Tekye Sabastian Ivey-Jones, Kryshten Jordan Ivey-Jones

Thank you for continuing to love me through my challenging times. I am confident in that you receive the revelation knowledge of **"The Light"** that the **"Word"** illuminates from the Holy Bible pages. May **"The Light"** shine through you so bright, that you and others may always see the reflection of the spirit that is the authentic you! **I pray you continue to find fulfillment in your quest for any answers you seek. "The Light is the only way to <u>find</u> that life you were born to live, and the only way to live <u>through</u> a truly happy, productive & prosperous life.**
May we together reign with Jesus forever!

~~ I Love You! ~~
Always & Forever
Ma'mah
2012

Thank you to the AuthorHouse Team!

THE KEY POINTS!

Tracing the Family of Noah
and
Understanding The Blessing of Abraham

The Book of
GENESIS

Based on "The Message Bible" by Eugene H. Peterson
Adapted and Written by Joyful Lady Faye Ivey-Jones
Completed: Sunday, February 18, 2007

GENESIS

Tracing the Family of Noah
and
Understanding The Blessing of Abraham

Noah had Shem, Ham and Japheth and died after the flood at 950 years old.

Noah had Shem, after many generations came Nahor who had Terah:

Terah had Abram, Nahor and Haran. Haran had Lot and Micah before he died.

Nahor married his niece, Haran's daughter Milcah; they had Bethuel who had Rebekah and Laban.

Abram raised his brother Haran's son Lot. Abram married Sarai and together they had Isaac. Abram also had Ishmael by Sarai's handmaiden Hagar. Ishmael had 12 sons.

Isaac married his uncle Nahor's granddaughter Rebekah, and together they had Esau and Jacob.

Esau married Canaan women out of spite and had 5 sons.

Jacob married Rachel (Laban's daughter) and together they had Joseph and Benjamin.

Jacob together with Rachel's Handmaiden Bilhah had 2 sons.

Jacob also married Rachel's sister Leah who gave him 6 sons and a daughter. Zilpah had 2 sons.

Joseph married Asenath and together they had Manasseh and Ephraim.

Sons of **Terah**
Abram, Nahor, Haran

Sons of **Abram /Abraham**
Ishmael

Isaac

Sons of Ishmael				Sons of Isaac
Nebaioth	Mibsam	Massa	Jetur	Esau
Kedar	Mishma	Hadad	Naphish	**Jacob**
Adbeel	Dumah	Tema	Kedemah	

The 12 sons of Jacob
(Born in Paddan Aram)

The 12 Tribes of Israel

Sons by **Leah**	Sons by **Rachael**		
Reuben	Joseph		Reuben
Simeon	Benjamin		Simeon
Levi			Epphraim (Joseph's son accepted by Israel)
Judah	Sons by Bilhah (Rachel's Handmaiden)		Manasseh (Joseph's son adopted by Israel)
Issachar	Dan		Benjamin
Zebulum	Naphtali		Judah
Dinah (Daughter)			Issachar
			Zebulum
			Dan
Sons by Zilpah (Leah's Handmaiden)			Naphatali
Gad			Gad
Asher			Asher

Wives and Sons of Esau
Adah had Eliphaz   Basemath had Reuel   Oholibamah had Jeush, Jalam and Korah

GENESIS

(Refer to your bible for completion)

GOD, in the beginning created the Heavens and Earth and all that you see and all that you don't see. God spoke into existence light out of darkness, the firmament, the waters, the seed-bearing plants, the sea-life, the birds and all types of cattle, reptiles and bugs. God saw that it was good and then created man in His own image. God called him Adam, and gave him dominion over everything on earth and told him to be fruitful and multiply. God saw that everything was good, then seeing that man needed a companion God created woman. Adam thanked Him and named her Eve. God placed Adam and Eve in the Garden of Eden with expectations for them to live a full and beautiful life in paradise. But evil temptation entered the garden and the fall of man began. God expelled Adam and Eve from the Garden of Eden and sent them to work the ground. Adam and Eve then had 2 sons, Cain and Abel. After some time Cain slew Abel. God then sent Cain from His presence to live in the wilderness. Cain and his wife gave birth to Enoch and the generations followed. When Adam was 103 years old he and Eve gave birth to another son and called him Seth. At age 105, Seth then had a son whom he called Enosh. Men and women now began praying and worshiping God. After having many sons and daughters Seth died at age 912. The generations continued.

Now Noah was a good man of integrity who walked with God. Noah had 3 sons: Shem, Ham and Japheth. God was displeased that the earth had become a sewer with violence everywhere and the people corrupt and life corrupt to the core. God told Noah to build a ship because he was going to destroy every living thing. He gave him very specific instructions on its structure and dimensions. God then told Noah to take his wife and family with him, including every kind of bird, mammal and reptile was to be loaded onto the ship. (Gen. 1-6)

Who were the sons of Adam and Eve?

What was the first thing God gave Adam?

Who were the sons of Noah?

How old was Noah when he had his first son?

2

What did God tell Noah to load on the ship besides his family and the animals?

```

```

God told Noah to now board the ship because he was the only righteous one. Again he told him to take his family and instructed him to take female and male of clean and unclean animals. Noah was obedient. He was 600 years old when the flood began. (Gen. 7)

Why was God displeased?

```


```

After 150 days, God caused the winds to blow and the water began to recede. The ship came to rest on the Ararat mountain range. The flood subsided and Noah tested for dry land. When Noah was 601 years old, the flood waters dried up. God spoke to Noah and told him when to leave the ark. He disembarked and built an altar and made a burnt-offering sacrifice to God. God promised He would never again kill off every living thing as He had done. (Gen. 8)

Where did the ship finally come to rest?

```

```

What was the purpose for sending out the Raven?

```


```

How did Noah know that the floods had subsided and how old was he at that time?

```


```

What did God say would never cease?

```


```

God told Noah to replenish the earth. He said "Do not be afraid, all beast and fowl will fear you." He told him what he had provided for food and promised by covenant, to every living thing, never to destroy again. He gave them a sign of His Covenant. (Gen. 9)

What kind of animals could Noah eat?

```

```

What was the sign of the covenant?

```

```

This chapter lists in detail the grandsons of Noah. (Gen. 10)

Who were the sons of Shem?

```

```

As the people came to settle in Shinar, they decided to build a city and a tower that would reach heaven. God thought they would stop at nothing so He garbled their speech so they wouldn't understand each other and then scattered them all over the world. Two years after the flood, Noah's son Shem was 100 years old and had Arphaxad and died at age 600.
Arphaxad had Shelah and died at 438 years old.
Shelah had Eber and also died at 438 years old.
Eber had Peleg and died at 464 years old.
Peleg had Reu and died at 244 years old.
Reu had Serug and died at 239 years old.
Serug had Nahor and died at 230 years old.
Nahor had Terah and died at 148 years old.
Terah had Abram, Nahor and Haran and died at 205 years old.
Terah, a descendent of Noah, Shem and Nahor, was the father of Abram. They set out from Ur of the Chaldees for the land of Canaan, but settled in Haran. Terah died there at age 205. (Gen. 11)

Why did the people want to build a city and a tower to reach heaven?

```

```

How many generations were there from Noah to Abram?

```

```

Which one of Noah's sons, did the generational blessing pass through?

```

```

God then told Abram, at age 75, to leave his country, family and father's home for a land that He will show him. God promised to make Abram a great nation. So Abram left and took his wife Sarai, and his nephew Lot went with him. Abram passed through the country as far as Shechem and the Oak of Moreh which were occupied by the Canaanites. God appeared to Abram, and told him to build an altar at the place He had appeared to him. Abram moved on and pitched his tent between Bethel to the west and Ai to the east, where he built an altar and prayed to God. He finally ended up in Negev. Abram, now moved near Egypt because of the famine, and told his wife to say she was his sister for fear that he would be killed because she was so beautiful and men would desire her. Pharaoh took her to live with him.

Because of Sarai, Abram got along very well and accumulated much wealth. But God punished Pharaoh by making everybody sick, because he had Abram's wife. Pharaoh confronted Abram about this then returned his wife to him. Abram then had to leave the country. He went back to Negev. (Gen. 12)

What land did God tell Abram He would give him and his children?

Where did Abram go during the time of the famine?

Why did Pharaoh make Abram and Sarai get out of the country?

The wealth that Abram and Lot accumulated was too much for the land they occupied and they mutually separated to their own lands. Lot took the plain of Jordan, near Sodom, and Abram settled in Canaan. Abram pitched his tent by the Oaks of Mamre in Hebron. There he built an altar to God. (Gen. 13)

Why did Abram and Lot separate?

Four kings: Amraphel, Arioch, Kedorlaomer and Tidal, went off to fight five kings: Bera, Birsha, Shinab, Shemeber, Zoar, and defeated them. They captured Lot and all his belongings. When Abram heard of this, he organized his army from his household and defeated the four kings. He recaptured Lot, all his belongings and returned the people and their belongings to King Bera of Sodom, who thanked him.

Abram refused any reward from the king of Sodom. **MELCHIZEDEK,** King of Salem, who was the **HIGH PRIEST**, brought out bread and wine and blessed Abram. Abram then gave Melchizedek, 1/10th of the recovered plunder. (Gen. 14)

Why were the kings at war?

| |
| |
| |

How did the kings of Sodom and Gomorrah get captured?

| |
| |
| |

After Abram won the battle, what type of celebration do you think they had?

| |
| |
| |

Who was Melchizedek?

| |
| |
| |

God again appeared to Abram, reminding him of God's promise. Abram made sacrifice and God blessed him and revealed to him the land that he would be given; the land from the Nile River in Egypt to the River Euphrate in Assyria, the country of the Kenites, Kenizzites, Kadmonities, Hittites, Perizzites, Rephaim, Amorites, Canaanites, Girgashites and Jebusites. (Gen. 15)

Which generation did God say would return to the land He promised?

| |

Sarai was now anxious to have a child and encouraged Abram to mate with Hagar her handmaiden. Together they produced a son named Ishmael, Abram was age 86. Sarai quickly began to resent Hagar because of the condescending treatment she was receiving. Sarai became abusive to Hagar and Hagar ran away. God comforted her in the dessert and told her to go back and that she would have a son and to name him Ishmael. He also told her He would give her a big family, children past counting. He also told her what the nature/character of this child would be. (Gen. 16).

6

How did God describe the character of Hagar's son to be born?

When Abram was 99 years old, God told him that he would now have a son and become the father of many nations. God made a covenant with him and told him his name is now Abraham, and his wife's name would now become Sarah. He gave to him and his descendents the whole country of Canaan to own forever and said He would be their God. He than gave instructions on honoring the covenant for generations to come. Now Abraham 99 years old, and his 13 year old son Ishmael, were circumcised. (Gen. 17)

What did God tell Abraham he must do to honor the covenant for generations to come?

One day after God appeared to Abraham, he saw three men standing before him. Abraham welcomed them in and made them comfortable with water to wash their feet and with the help of Sarah and the servants, made a meal to eat. One of the men said "This time next year, Sarah will have a son." Sarah overheard in disbelief. God settled on Abraham as the one to train his children and future family to observe God's way of life; to live kindly and generously and fairly so that God could complete in Abraham what he promised him. God told Abraham of His plans to go to Sodom. Abraham challenged God on His decision concerning Sodom and Gomorrah, so God agreed not to destroy that land if He could find 10 decent people living there. (Gen. 18)

Why did God pick Abraham as the one to be the recipient of His Blessing?

Why did Sarah laugh at the news Abraham received from the visitors?

What was Abraham's concern about the people of Sodom and Gomorrah?

God's angels arrived to survey the land and were met at the gate by Abraham's nephew Lot. Lot invited the men to rest at his house during their stay. When the towns-people heard of this, they wanted to have their way with the men, but Lot protected them. The men (who were angels) told Lot to get out of that land and take every one of his family members with him and not to look back, for they were going to destroy that land. Lot obeyed, but his wife out of curiosity, looked back and was immediately turned into a pillar of salt. God destroyed that land, blasted it off the face of the earth, but was mindful of Abraham and spared his nephew. Lot soon went to live with his daughters in the mountains where Moab, the ancestor of the present-day Moabites, and BeneAmmi, the ancestor of the present-day Ammonites, were born. (Gen. 19).

What comment made Abraham confront God?

| |
| |

Why did Lot have to flee his home?

| |
| |

What happened to Lot at his daughter's house?

| |
| |

Abraham traveled to Negev and settled down between Kedesh and Shur. While camping in Gerar, he pretended that Sarah was his sister. Abimelech, king of Gerar, sent for Sarah and took her. But God came to Abimelech in a dream and told him she was married. Having no idea he was doing anything wrong, God encouraged him to return Sarah to her husband, and spared the king. The king also gave to Abraham gifts and invited them to live anywhere on his land they desired. (Gen. 20)

How did Abimelech find out that Sarah was Abraham's wife?

| |
| |

Abraham and Sarah gave birth to Isaac. When he was 8 days old, Abraham circumcised him just as God commanded. Sarah became very annoyed when Ishmael taunted baby Isaac. She refused to have Hagar and Ishmael live there any longer. So Abraham made them leave. In her despair, God comforted her and made provision for them in the dessert. Ishmael grew up and married an Egyptian woman. Abraham made a peace covenant with Abimelech and lived in Philistine country for a long time. (Gen. 21)

How old was Abraham when Sarah gave birth to Isaac?

Now God tested Abraham by instructing him to take his son Isaac to Moriah and sacrifice him as a burnt offering. Abraham proceeded in obedience, but God halted him and rewarded him for his obedience. Abraham gathered his things and settled in Beersheba. (Gen. 22)

Why didn't Abraham carry out the burnt-offering sacrifice of his son?

Sarah died at the age of 127 years. Abraham purchased the cave and the field at Machpelah from Ephron, son of Zohar, for a burial plot for his wife Sarah, and paid 400 silver shekels with the town council of Hittites as witnesses. That's how the Ephron's field next to Mamre—its cave and all the trees within its borders (present day Hebron) in the land of Canaan went from the possession of Hittites to Abraham's property as a burial plot. (Gen. 23)

Who insisted on paying for the land where the burial plot would be?

As Abraham was getting older, he asked his servant to go to his hometown and bring back a wife for his son Isaac. The servant set out to do what was asked of him. He met Rebekah, the grand-niece of Abraham. She was beautiful, kind and a virgin. After several days, Rebekah and her maids followed Abraham's servant back home where she met and married Isaac. Abraham was pleased. (Gen. 24)

What did Abraham tell his servant to request of the prospective wife of Isaac?

What was the reply that would be the sign?

Although Abraham married again to Keturah and had 6 more sons, He gave all that he possessed to his son Isaac. While he was still alive, he gave gifts to the sons he had with his other concubines and sent them away to put distance between them and Isaac. Abraham at 175 years old, was buried next to Sarah by his sons. Ishmael died at age 137, leaving 12 sons who didn't get along with any of their kin and they settled down all the way along Havilah near Egypt, eastward to Shur, in the direction of Assyria. They are known as the Ishmaelites.

At age 40, Isaac, married Rebekah the Aramean of Paddan Aram, the sister of Laban. She had a very difficult pregnancy and sought God, who told her she was carrying two nations in her womb. She gave birth to twins. (Esau and Jacob). Esau shrugged off his rights as the first-born for a meal that Jacob had prepared. (Gen. 25)

Why do you think Abraham separated Isaac from his concubines' sons?

Isaac and Rebekah gave birth to two sons. Who was the oldest?

Give your best estimate of how much older he was?

There was a famine and Isaac went down to Abimelech, king of the Philistines in Gerar. God appeared and told him not to travel to Egypt but instructed him to stay there. God told him that He is giving them all the land and would provide for them, fulfilling the oath he swore to Abraham. Isaac obeyed.

Just like his father Abraham's wife Sarah, his wife Rebekah, was very beautiful, so to those men who questioned him about her, he told them she was his sister. Abimelech saw him fondling her and asked him why did he say she was his sister? Abimelech then gave orders that no one was to touch her.

Isaac planted crops and became very wealthy. The Philistines became envious and began to sabotage the wells that his father Abraham had dug in his day. King Abimelech, aware of the increasing wealth, asked Isaac to leave the land. Isaac left and settled in the valley of Gerar and began digging out the wells that were sabotaged by the Philistines. Every attempt he made the Philistines came and argued with him over the well. Finally, he dug a well without any resistance from anyone and God appeared to him to assure him that He was with him. Sensing that God was with Isaac, Abimelech came to Isaac with his advisor Ahuzzath and Phicol the head of his troops. Isaac inquired of their presence knowing that they had thrown him out of their country. They wanted to make a deal, a covenant of friendly relationships. Isaac prepared a feast; they exchanged oaths and parted friends. The next morning Issac's servant informed him they had struck water in the new well. At age 40, Esau married two Hittite women. These daughters-in-law, turned out to be thorns in the sides of Isaac and Rebekah. (Gen. 26)

What situation has now re-occurred again in this chapter?

Give your best description of the correlation between these situations.

Why do you think Abimelech was so fearful?

When Isaac became an old man and was nearly blind, he called Esau and asked him to prepare a meal and bring it so that he could bless him before he died. Overhearing this, Rebekah plotted and instructed Jacob on what to do so he would receive the blessing. They succeeded, and Esau was furious. He decided that he would kill his brother after his father's death. When Rebekah heard of this, she sent Jacob to Haran to live with her brother Laban, until Esau cooled down. (Gen. 27)

Describe the scheme that tricked Isaac.

Isaac blessed him and sent him off and reminded him not to marry any daughters of the Canaan. When Esau heard of this, he went and married one of Ishmael's daughters on spite. Jacob traveled and at night camped. He laid his head on a stone and God appeared to him in a dream, promising to stick with him. The next morning he arose, using the stone that he used as a pillow, erected it as a memorial to God, poured oil over it and made a vow to God. (Gen. 28)

What was the vow Jacob made to God?

Jacob traveled on and came upon women waiting for other women to come to assist with the moving of the stone that covered the well where they watered their sheep. As Rachel approached, Jacob saw her beauty and rolled away the stone single-handedly. He introduced himself and she told her father Laban, who came to meet him. They welcomed him into their home. Jacob worked for Laban for 14 years to marry Rachel. Together they gave birth to Joseph. But because of customs he had to first marry her sister Leah. They had 4 sons. (Gen. 29)

How many years total did Jacob work for Laban?

Rachel was jealous of her sister and angry because her womb was closed. So she gave Jacob her handmaiden to bear a child. She gave him 2 sons. Her sister Leah now became jealous and gave to Jacob her handmaiden who bore 2 sons. Leah then gave birth to 2 more sons. God then opened Rachel's womb and she had a son, they named him Joseph. Jacob now wanted to go home and take his family and possessions. He made a deal with Laban to divide the wealth. (Gen. 30)

What did Reuben bring from the field to give to his mother?

What are mandrakes?

Jacob experienced ill treatment coming from Laban, and God told him to go back home where he was born and that He would be with him. Laban cheated Jacob over and over again but God always turned the evil into good and blessed him. Jacob told Rachel and Leah what God had told him. They agreed to leave. Rachel stole her father's household gods and packed them as Jacob rounded up his family and flock. Three days later Laban received word that Jacob was gone and went after him. Seven days later he caught up with him and accused him of stealing his daughters, his grandchildren, his flock and his household gods. Jacob knew nothing of the missing gods and invited Laban to search for anything that belonged to him and said, if he found that any one there had them that person dies. Unable to find any of his property, sorrowfully Laban defended himself and wanted to settle things by making a covenant between them. (Gen. 31)

Why was Laban unable to find the household gods?

Who do you think Jacob's curse affected? How?

As Jacob traveled homeward he received word that his brother was approaching and Jacob was afraid. So he sent 3 servants ahead with gifts for Esau at intervals to soften him before the meeting. During the night he wrestled all night with a man who, seeing that Jacob wouldn't give up, threw Jacob's hip out of socket. But Jacob wouldn't give up until the man blessed him. Jacob realized he had seen God and lived to tell it. (Gen. 32)

In the Jewish tradition, why is eating the hip muscle forbidden?

Then Jacob saw his brother approaching. The meeting between Jacob and Esau united them and forgiveness was expressed and received. Esau met all of Jacob's family and they planned to meet again. Esau headed for Seir and Jacob for Succoth. Jacob arrived in Shechem in the land of Canaan all the way from Paddan Aram. He purchased the land where he pitched his tent from Hamor the father of Shechem, for 100 silver coins and built an altar to God. (Gen. 33)

What is interesting about the order in which Jacob presented his family to his brother Esau?

Why do you think he did that?

Jacob's daughter Dinah on her way to visit friends was raped by Shechem the son of Hamor the Hivite. He fell so in love with her that he wanted to marry her. He asked his father to get her as his wife. Jacob and his sons were angry upon learning of what happened. Shechem and Hamor were led to believe that the marriage would be agreed if they would get circumcised. So, all the men in town were circumcised. While they were all healing, Jacob's sons, Levi and Simeon killed every man in town in retaliation for treating their sister like a whore. (Gen. 34)

When Hamor spoke with Jacob, what did he mean by intermarry with us?

God Spoke to Jacob. "Go back to Bethel. Stay there and build an altar to the God who revealed Himself to you when you were running for your life from your brother Esau." Jacob informed his family and told then to rid themselves of all alien gods, bathe and put on clean clothes. As they traveled out, paralyzing fear came over all the surrounding villages making them unable to pursue the sons of Jacob.

Jacob and his company arrived in Bethel and built an altar there to worship. God appeared and blessed Jacob and told him his name was no longer Jacob but Israel, and that he would now have the land that was given to Abraham and Isaac and would be passed on to his descendants. Right there where God spoke, Jacob set a stone pillar, poured a drink-offering and anointed it with oil. They left Bethel and headed for Ephrath. Rachel went into hard labor, named the boy Benoni and died. Jacob/Israel named him Benjamin. Jacob/Israel buried her in Bethlehem. Reuben defiled his father's marriage bed. Jacob/Israel finally made it back home to his father Isaac. (Hebron) Isaac died at 180 years old and was buried with his family. His sons Esau and Jacob buried him. (Gen. 35)

What was the charge or blessing that God gave to Jacob after naming him Israel?

| |
| |

What sin did Reuben commit?

| |
| |

The family of Esau is also called Edom. He married women of Canaan: Adah, Oholibamah, and Basemath. Esau and Jacob both had possession too many to dwell together. The land couldn't support the herds of livestock. So Esau settled in the hill country of Seir. (Gen. 36)

Name the wives and sons of Esau.

| |
| |

Joseph was 17 years old and the favorite son of Israel. He was hated by his brothers because of his dreams he revealed to them. Israel sent Joseph to check on the progress of his brothers as they pastured the flock. He brought back bad reports. When the brothers saw him approaching, they plotted to kill him and tell their father he had been eaten by wild animals. Reuben intervened and forbid his brothers to kill Joseph. The brothers ripped off the beautiful coat Israel had made for Joseph and threw him into a dry cistern. Along came a caravan of Ishmaelites on their way to Egypt to sell their wares. The brothers all decided to sell their brother for 20 silver coins. He was then sold again to Potiphar who managed Pharaoh's household in Egypt. Reuben sought Joseph without success. The brothers butchered a goat and covered Joseph's coat with its blood and took it to their father as evidence of the death of Joseph. Jacob/Israel grieved deeply. (Gen. 37)

Why was Joseph, Jacob's favorite son?

Judah met a Canaanite woman named Shua and had 3 sons, Er, Onan and Shelah. Judah's son Er, married Tamar but he died after grievously offending God. Judah's son Onan, died also from sin. Judah slept with who he thought was a prostitute. She kept proof he left behind which ultimately exposed his sin. (Gen. 38)

What was the sin that Judah's son committed?

What act did Judah try to hide?

What was the evidence that tied Judah to this act?

Joseph became the assistant to Potiphar, because of his good work. He was thrown into jail because Potiphar's wife lied and said he tried to have his way with her because he refused her. But God continued to be with him. God gave him favor with the head jailer who in turn put Joseph in charge of the whole operation (Gen. 39)

What was the proof Potiphar's wife produced to support her accusations?

Pharaoh had his cupbearer and baker thrown in jail for crossing him. Joseph interpreted their dreams and asked the cupbearer to remember him when he was reinstated to his normal position for duty under Pharaoh. (Gen. 40)

Describe the dream that was asked to be interpreted by:

    a. The cupbearer.

b. The baker.

Two years later, Pharaoh had dreams that he couldn't understand. He sent for the magicians and sages of Egypt but they couldn't interpret his dreams. At that moment the head cupbearer who had been reinstated to his position remembered Joseph had interpreted his dream accurately, he told Pharaoh of him who sent for Joseph immediately. Joseph told Pharaoh, it would be God who interprets your dream. Pharaoh told Joseph of the 3 dreams and Joseph interpreted them, warning him of the famine to come. Pharaoh was impressed and appointed Joseph in charge of the entire country of Egypt. Pharaoh, adorned him, renamed him Zaphenath-Peneah, and gave him Potiphar's daughter Asenath, as his wife. They had two sons, Manasseh and Ephraim. Joseph accumulated an abundant surplus of grain during the seven years. When the famine came, Egypt was the only country that had bread. Pharaoh told all the people in distress to go to Joseph and do whatever he told them to do, for Joseph was in charge of the land and the sale of grain. Soon the whole world was coming to buy grain from Joseph. (Gen. 41)

Describe Pharaoh's dream.

When Jacob/Israel learned that there was food in Egypt, he sent 10 of his sons there to buy food. He did not send Benjamin for fear that something would happen to him. Joseph's brothers didn't recognize him but bowed and honored him as master. Joseph did recognize his brothers but treated them as strangers. He treated them roughly and threw them in jail for 3 days, telling them they were spies. Joseph overheard their discussion acknowledging that the treatment they were receiving was due to the way they treated their brother. Joseph cried. He then thought up a scheme to send food home for his family. Joseph tied up Simeon while the brothers watched and then ordered that their bags be filled with grain and their money put back in their sacks. When the brothers traveled for home and stopped at night to camp, they found that their money had been put back in their sacks. They became puzzled and frightened. Upon arriving home, they told their father how the master had kept Simeon, and sent them home with grain and their money telling them to return with their youngest brother. (Gen. 42)

Why did Benjamin have to return to Egypt with is brothers?

How did Reuben try to convince his father to comply?

After all the grain was gone and starvation was inevitable Israel gave in and allowed the brothers to take Benjamin with them back to Egypt to get more grain. When Joseph saw the brothers arrive with Benjamin, he told his house steward to take them in the house and make them at home; they would eat with him at noon. The men were afraid. At dinner, Joseph asked about their father and was told he is well. They all feasted well. They were served from Joseph's table. (Gen. 43)

What did Israel tell his sons to take with them to Egypt?

How did Judah convince his father to comply?

Joseph then ordered the house stewards to again fill their bags with grain and put their money back in their sacks, and also to put his silver chalice in the bag of the youngest brother. As the men set off to journey home, Joseph instructed the steward to go after them and make search for the silver chalice and bring back the one who has it. The steward did as he asked. The brothers returned and begged Joseph to allow Benjamin to go free. (Gen. 44)

Explain how and why Joseph plotted the "chalice recovery" scheme?

Which brother begged Joseph for Benjamin's release?

Joseph, full of emotion, sent all his attendants out of the room and then identified himself to his brothers. The Egyptians overheard his sobbing and reported it to Pharaoh. Joseph then told his brothers that it was God and not them who sent him to Egypt. He told them how God's plan was for him to be the head of Egypt and prepare for the famine so that his family could eat. He told them to go home and bring everyone they were connected with and he would make sure they wanted for nothing. Pharaoh was glad that Joseph's brothers had come. He agreed, tell them to come and they will eat off the fat of the land. Pharaoh sent them off with wagons to bring the children, wives and their father. He also sent sufficient grain for the trip and gave them all new clothes. Israel was elated and was anxious to see Joseph. (Gen. 45)

How did Pharaoh react to the news about Joseph's family?

| |
| |
| |

Israel set out on the journey with everything he owned. He arrived at Beersheba and worshiped, offering sacrifices to the God of his father Isaac. God spoke to him and comforted him. They continued on to Egypt. The meeting between Jacob and Joseph was very emotional. Jacob and his sons in Egypt totaled 70, (not counting the wives of his sons). (Gen. 46)

What did God promise Jacob/Israel, as His final act in Jacob's life?

| |
| |
| |

Why did Joseph want his family to dwell in the land of Goshen?

| |
| |
| |

Joseph took 5 of his brothers to meet Pharaoh. Pharaoh welcomed them and gave them the choice land of Goshen (the land of Rameses) as they requested. He also told Joseph to give them work, taking care of his livestock. Joseph then took his father and introduced him to Pharaoh. Israel, now 130 years old, blessed Pharaoh and left.

As time went on, because of the famine, eventually there was no food anywhere. The people had no more money. They had paid it all to Joseph for food. In despair, the people begged for food. Joseph then accepted their livestock as payment for food. The following year, the people again begged for food, this time offering the only thing they had left, their bodies and farms. They offered to be slaves to Pharaoh, give up their land and work for him in return for food so they wouldn't starve to death. Joseph had now bought up all the farms in Egypt for Pharaoh (except from the Priests). That's how Pharaoh wound of owning all the land and having the people as slaves. Now that Pharaoh owned all the land and the slaves, Joseph announced to the people that he would give them seed to plant the ground and from the harvest they would give to

Pharaoh 1/5 of the crops and 4/5 they could keep to feed their families. The people were grateful to Joseph for saving their lives. They were glad to be slaves to Pharaoh. Joseph decreed *A Fifth Goes to Pharaoh*, as a law (with the exception of the Priests). Now at 147 years old, Israel asked Joseph to take him out of Egypt when he died to bury him alongside his fathers. Joseph promised. (Gen. 47)

Why didn't Joseph buy the lands belonging to the Priests?

| |
| |
| |

When Joseph was told that his father was ill, he took his two sons Manasseh and Ephraim, and went to see him. Jacob/Israel told Joseph how God had blessed him to pass on the blessing. He also told Joseph that he was adopting Joseph's 2 sons he had while in Egypt to share in equal portion of the inheritance. Israel then kissed and embraced them then blessed them and presented to Joseph as the first among his brothers, the ridge of land he had taken from the Amorites with his sword and bow. (Gen. 48)

What was God's blessing, as revealed to Joseph by Jacob before he died?

| |
| |
| |

Jacob called his sons to tell them what they could expect in the days ahead.

He renounced Reuben as the top in honor and power because he climbed into his father's marriage bed.

He scolded Simeon and Levi, wanting nothing to do with their vendettas or bitter feuds, because they killed men in fits of temper, he cursed their uncontrolled anger.

He likened Judah to a lion's cub, crouched like a lion, king of the beasts who will keep the scepter and keep firm grip on the command staff until the ultimate ruler comes.

He said Zebulun settles down and is a safe harbor for ships alongside Sidon.

He said Issachar is one tough donkey and when he saw how good and pleasant the country was, he gave up his freedom and went to work as a slave.

He said Dan will handle matters of justice for his people. He is a lethal serpent in ambush by the road.

He said Gad will be attacked by bandits, but he will trip them up.

He said Asher will become famous for rich foods, candies and sweets fit for the kings.

He said Naphtali is a deer running free that gives birth to lovely fawns.

He said Joseph is a wild spirited donkey by a spring on a hill, held steady under fire of hate-tipped arrows. With the backing of the Champion of Jacob, may He help you! May the blessings of your father exceed the blessings of the ancient mountains and surpass the delights of the eternal hills: May they rest on the head of Joseph, on the brow of the one consecrated among his brothers.

He said Benjamin is a ravenous wolf. All morning he gorges on his kill, at evening divides up what's left over.

He then instructed them to bury him with his fathers in the cave, in the field of Ephron the Hittite, the cave in the field of Machpelah facing Mamre in the land of Canaan, the field Abraham bought from Ephron the Hittite for a burial plot. Buried there are Abraham and Sarah; Isaac and Rebekah and also Leah. He then pulled his feet into bed and breathe is last breath and was gathered to his people. (Gen. 49)

What do you think about the things Israel spoke over each son's life?

Joseph wept over his father and kissed him. He then instructed the physicians in his employ to embalm him which took 40 days. There was 70 days of public mourning by the Egyptians. Joseph was granted permission by Pharaoh to bury his father in Canaan. Arriving at the Atad threshing floor just across the Jordan River, they stopped for a 7 day mourning period, letting their grief out in loud and lengthy lament. Israel was then taken to be buried in the plot Abraham bought from Ephron the Hittite.
The brothers were now afraid that Joseph was carrying a grudge and feared he would pay them back for what they had done to him. So, they sent a message telling Joseph that before their father's death, he gave a command to tell Joseph to forgive your brothers' sin. When Joseph received their message, he wept. They came to him and threw themselves on the ground before him and said, "We will be your slaves". Joseph replied, "Don't be afraid." He told them the evil they did to him God used those same plans for good. Joseph lived to 110 years old. He told them God would visit them and take them out of that land and back to the land that He promised Abraham, Isaac and Jacob. He asked them to take his bones with them. He was embalmed and placed in a coffin in Egypt. (Gen. 50)

What is your opinion of Joseph?

| |
| |
| |
| |

What is the "Blessing of Abraham?

| |
| |
| |
| |

Name_____Date_____

THE KEY POINTS!
GENESIS
Bible Review Quiz

Gen.1-6   Who were the sons of Adam and Eve?

What was the first thing God gave Adam?

Who were the sons of Noah?

How old was Noah when he had his first son?

What did God tell Noah to load on the ship besides his family & animals?

Gen. 7   Why was God displeased?

Gen. 8   Where did the ship finally come to rest?

What was the purpose for sending out the Raven?

How did Noah know that the floods had subsided and how old was he at that time?

| |
| |

What did God say would never cease?

| |
| |

Gen. 9   What kind of animals could Noah eat?

| |

What was the sign of the covenant?

| |

Gen. 10   Who were the sons of Shem?

| |

Gen. 11   Why did the people want to build a city and a tower to reach heaven?

| |
| |

How many generations were there from Noah to Abraham?

| |

Which one of Noah's sons, did the generational blessing pass through?

| |

Gen. 12   What land did God tell Abram He would give him and his children?

| |

Where did Abram go during the time of the famine?

| |

Why did Pharaoh make Abram and Sarai get out of the country?

_____

_____

Gen. 13   Why did Abram and Lot separate?

_____

_____

Gen. 14   Why were the kings at war?

_____

_____

How did the kings of Sodom and Gomorrah get captured?

_____

_____

After Abram won the battle, what type of celebration do you think
they had?

_____

_____

Who was Melchizedek?

_____

_____

Gen. 15   Which generation did God say would return to the land He promised?

_____

Gen. 16   How did God describe the character of Hagar's son to be born?

_____

_____

Gen. 17   What did God tell Abraham he must do to honor the covenant for
generations to come?

_____

_____

Gen. 18   Why did Sarah laugh at the news Abraham received from the visitors?

| |
| |

What was Abraham's concern about the people of Sodom and Gomorrah?

| |
| |

Gen. 19   What comment made Abraham confront God?

| |
| |

Why did Lot have to flee his home?

| |
| |

What happened to Lot at his daughter's house?

| |
| |

Gen. 20   How did Abimelech find out that Sarah was Abraham's wife?

| |
| |

Gen. 21   How old was Abraham when Sarah gave birth to Isaac?

| |
| |

Gen. 22   Why didn't Abraham carry out the burnt-offering sacrifice of his son?

| |
| |

Gen. 23   Who insisted on paying for the land where the burial plot would be?

| |

Gen. 24   What did Isaac tell his servant to request of the prospective wife of Isaac?

| |
| |

What was the reply that would be the sign?

| |
| |

Gen. 25   Why do you think Abraham separated Isaac from his concubines' sons?

| |
| |

Isaac and Rebekah gave birth to two sons. Who was the oldest?

| |

Give your best estimate of how much older he was?

| |

Gen. 26   What situation has now re-occurred again in this chapter?

| |
| |

Give your best description of the correlation between these situations.

| |
| |

Why do you think Abimelech was so fearful?

| |
| |

Gen. 27   Describe the scheme that tricked Isaac.

| |
| |

Gen. 28   What was the vow Jacob made to God?

Gen. 29   How many years total did Jacob work for Laban?

Gen. 30   What did Reuben bring from the field to give to his mother?

What are mandrakes?

Gen. 31   Why was Laban unable to find the household gods?

Who do you think Jacob's curse affected? How?

Gen. 32   In the Jewish tradition, why is eating the hip muscle forbidden?

Gen. 33   What is interesting about the order in which Jacob presented his family to his brother Esau? Why do you think he did that?

Gen. 34   When Hamor spoke with Jacob, what did he mean by intermarry with us?

Gen. 35   What was the charge or blessing that God gave to Jacob after naming him Israel?

| |
| |
| |

What sin did Reuben commit?

| |
| |
| |

Gen. 36   Name the wives and sons of Esau.

| |
| |
| |

Gen. 37   Why was Joseph, Jacob's favorite son?

| |
| |
| |

Gen. 38   What was the sin that Judah's son committed?

| |
| |
| |

What act did Judah try to hide?

| |
| |
| |

What was the evidence that tied Judah to this act?

| |
| |
| |

Gen. 39   What was the proof Potiphar's wife produced to support her accusations?

| |
| |
| |

Gen. 40   Describe the dream that was asked to be interpreted by:
a. The cupbearer.

| |
| |
| |

b.   The baker.

Gen. 41   Describe Pharaoh's dream.

Gen. 42   Why did Benjamin have to return to Egypt with is brothers?

How did Reuben try to convince his father to comply?

Gen. 43   What did Israel tell his sons to take with them to Egypt?

How did Judah convince his father to comply?

Gen. 44   Explain how and why Joseph plotted the "chalice recovery" scheme?

Which brother begged Joseph for Benjamin's release?

Gen. 45   How did Pharaoh react to the news about Joseph's family?

Gen. 46   What did God promise Jacob, as His final act in Jacob's life?

| |
| |

Why did Joseph want his family to dwell in the land of Goshen?

| |
| |

Gen. 47   Why didn't Joseph buy the lands belonging to the Priests?

| |
| |

Gen. 48   What was God's blessing, as revealed to Joseph by Jacob before he died?

| |
| |

Gen. 49   What do you think about the things Israel spoke over each son's life?

| |
| |
| |
| |

Gen. 50   What is your opinion of Joseph?

| |
| |
| |
| |

The Key Points!

What is the Blessing of Abraham?

| |
| |
| |
| |

How does the Blessing of Abraham apply to your life today?

| |
| |
| |
| |

What can you do to assure the Blessing continues in your life?

| |
| |
| |
| |

GENESIS-1

<u>The Key Points!</u>

GENESIS

Bible Review Quiz—Answer Sheet

Gen. 6   Who were the sons of Adam and Eve? Cain, Abel and Seth.
What was the first thing God gave Adam? Dominion over everything on earth.
Who were the sons of Noah? Shem, Ham and Japheth
How old was Noah when he had his first son? 500 years old.
What did God tell Noah to load on the ship beside his family and animals? Food.

Gen. 7   Why was God displeased? Because of the corruption.

Gen. 8   Where did the ship finally come to rest? On the Ararat Mountain.
What was the purpose for sending out the Raven? To survey dry land.
How did Noah know that the floods had subsided and how old was he at that time? The dove returned with an olive branch. He was 601 yrs. old
What did God say would never cease? Planting and harvest, cold and heat, summer and winter, day and night.

Gen. 9   What kind of animals could Noah eat? The clean animals.
What was the sign of the covenant? The rainbow.

Gen. 10   Who were the sons of Shem? Elam. Asshur, Arphaxad, Lud and Aram.

Gen. 11   Why did the people want to build a city and a tower to reach heaven? They wanted to make themselves famous and prevent themselves from being scattered.
How many generations were there from Noah to Abraham? 10.
Which one of Noah's sons, did the generational blessing pass through? Shem

Gen. 12   What land did God tell Abram He would give him and his children? Canaan—(Shechem and the Oak of Moreh).
Where did Abram go during the time of the famine? Egypt.
Why did Pharaoh make Abram and Sarai get out of the country? Because he lied, pretending that Sarai was his sister. (God had stricken everyone in the palace with a serious illness.)

GENESIS-2

Gen. 13   Why did Abram and Lot separate? Because they both had much wealth and the land couldn't support this livestock.

Gen. 14   Why were the kings at war? Because the kings of Sodom, Gomorrah, Admah, Zeboiim and Bela revolted after being under the thumb of King Kedorlaomer for 12 years.
How did the kings of Sodom and Gomorrah get captured? When King Kedorlaomer and his allied kings conquered the whole region of the Amalekites and the Amorites, King Bera of Sodom and his allied kings, went against the enemy in the Valley of Siddim. The kings of Sodom and Gomorrah fell into the tar pits and were captured and all their people and possessions were taken.
After Abram won the battle, what type of celebration do you think they had? Communion.
Who was Melchizedek? King of Salem, Priest of the High God.

Gen. 15   Which generation did God say would return to the land He promised? 4th.

Gen. 16   How did God describe the character of Hagar's son to be born and what was is name? A bucking bronco, a real fighter, always getting into trouble. Ishmael

Gen. 17   What did God tell Abraham he must do to honor the covenant for generations to come? Get circumcised and the same for his sons.

Gen. 18   Why did Sarah laugh at the news Abraham received from the visitors? She thought she was too old be get pregnant and her husband too old to get her pregnant.
What was Abraham's concern about the people of Sodom and Gomorrah? The good people would suffer with the bad.

Gen. 19   What comment made Abraham confront God? That He would destroy the land as well as the people in Sodom and Gomorrah.
Why did Lot have to flee his home? Because that entire region would be destroyed.
What happened to Lot at his daughter's house? His daughters got him drunk and got themselves pregnant by him.

Gen. 20   How did Abimelech find out that Sarah was Abraham's wife? God revealed it to him in a dream.

Gen. 21   How old was Abraham when Sarah gave birth to Isaac? 100 yrs. old.

GENESIS-3

Gen. 22   Why didn't Abraham carry out the burnt-offering sacrifice of his son? Once God was convinced of his faithfulness, God provided himself a sacrifice, by placing a ram in the thicket.

Gen. 23   Who insisted on paying for the land where the burial plot would be? Abraham.

Gen. 24   What did Isaac tell his servant to request of the prospective wife of Isaac? Lower your jug and give me a drink.
What was the reply that would be the sign? Drink and also let me water your camel.

Gen. 25   Why do you think Abraham separated Isaac from his concubines' sons? Because Isaac was to be the heir of God's promise.
Isaac and Rebekah gave birth to two sons. Who was the oldest? Esau.
Give your best estimate of how much older he was? A few minutes, they were twins.

Gen. 26   What situation has now re-occurred again in this chapter? The husbands, (Abraham and Isaac who were father and son) pretending that their wives were their sisters to the same man Abimelech.
Give your best description of the correlation between these situations. Both wives were so beautiful that both husbands feared being killed by other men who desired their wives.
Why do you think Abimelech was so fearful? Because he remembered the dream and what God told him would happen to him if he took Abraham's wife Sarah.

Gen. 27   Describe the scheme that tricked Isaac. Rebekah prepared the stew just as her husband liked it and had Jacob to dress in his brother Esau's clothing to smell like him so he would received the blessing intended for Esau.

Gen. 28   What was the vow Jacob made to God? To return to God 1/10 of everything He gave to him.

Gen. 29   How many years total did Jacob work for Laban? 20 years

Gen. 30   What did Reuben bring from the field to give to his mother? Mandrakes
What are mandrakes? A poisonous herb, having a very short stem and a thick, often forked root thought to resemble the human form.

There are several kinds, all belonging to the nightshade family and native to southern Europe and Asia. The mandrake was formally used in medicine because of its emetic and narcotic properties. Eating the root was believed to aid in conceiving a child.

Gen. 31   Why was Laban unable to find the household gods? Because Rachel hid them in a camel sack and was sitting on them. She claimed you could not stand up because she had her period.
Who do you think Jacob's curse affected? His wife Rachel. How? Because he was unaware that she had stolen the household gods when he spoke a curse over whoever had them would die.

Gen. 32   In the Jewish tradition, why is eating the hip muscle forbidden? Because the angel threw Jacob's hip out of joint when he wrestled with him all night. He then demanded to receive a blessing.

Gen. 33   What is interesting about the order in which Jacob presented his family to his brother Esau? That he put the concubines and their children out front when he feared what his brother might do, and put Leah and her children next and Rachel and her children in the rear.
Why do you think he did that? Because he loved Rachel and Joseph the best.

Gen. 34   When Hamor spoke with Jacob, what did he mean by intermarry with us? For his sons to marry Jacob's daughters and Jacob's sons to marry Hamor's daughters and be one family.

Gen. 35   What was the charge or blessing that God gave to Jacob after naming him Israel? To have children and flourish; that nations would come to him; kings would come out of his loins; the land God gave to Abraham and Isaac, He would give to Jacob.
What sin did Reuben commit? He slept with his father's concubine Bilhah.

Gen. 36   Name the wives and sons of Esau. Adah, had Eliphaz, Basemath had Reuel; Oholihamah had Jesush, Jalam, and Korah.

Gen. 37   Why was Joseph, Jacob's favorite son? Because he was the son of his old age and was the son of Rachel who he loved so much.

Gen. 38   What was the sin that Judah's son committed? He spilled his semen on the ground instead of giving his dead brother's wife a child.

What act did Judah try to hide? Sleeping with his daughter-in-law who he thought was a prostitute.

What was the evidence that tied Judah to this act? His staff and personal seal-and-cord.

Gen. 39   What was the proof Potiphar's wife produced to support her false accusations? Joseph's coat.

Gen. 40   Describe the dream that was asked to be interpreted by: a) The cupbearer. There was a vine with 3 branches, with ripened clusters of grapes. He took the grapes and squeezed them into Pharaoh's cup and gave it to him. b) The baker. He saw 3 wicker baskets on his head, the top basket had assorted pastries and the birds were picking in it.

Gen. 41   Describe Pharaoh's dream. He was standing on the Nile and 7 healthy cows came up out of the river and grazed on the marsh grass, followed by 7 cows that were all skin and bones. They ate up the 7 healthy ones, after which they were still skin and bones. Then there were 7 ears of grain, full-bodied and lush growing out of a single stalk, followed by 7 ears shriveled, thin and dried which swallowed up the full ears.

Gen. 42   Why did Benjamin have to return to Egypt with is brothers? As proof that the brothers weren't lying to Joseph. Joseph told the brothers they were spies and he had to test their truthfulness. He threw them in jail for 3 days and then kept Simeon in jail and sent the others home to return with their younger brother to prove they had been telling the truth.

How did Reuben try to convince his father to comply? He gave his father permission to kill his two sons if he didn't return with Benjamin.

Gen. 43   What did Israel tell his sons to take with them to Egypt? Gifts for the man of the finest products they could find on the land; balm and honey, some spices and perfumes, some pistachios and almonds.

How did Judah convince his father to comply? He told him they wouldn't go to get more food unless they took Benjamin with them and he would take full responsibility, putting his own life on the line.

Gen. 44   Explain how and why Joseph plotted the "chalice recovery" scheme? As the brothers were ready to return home, Joseph had his steward fill each of their bags with food and the money they paid for the food. Into Benjamin's bag he had included his silver chalice. When the men had departed, Joseph sent his steward to follow them and search for the silver chalice. Thereby, capturing the one who had possession of it.

GENESIS-6

He wanted a reason the keep Benjamin, probably because that would make his father come to Egypt.
Which brother begged Joseph for Benjamin's release? Judah

Gen. 45   How did Pharaoh react to the news about Joseph's family? He was happy to hear about them and offered his assistance to bring them to Egypt.

Gen. 46   What did God promise Jacob, as His final act in Jacob's life? That God would return Jacob to Canaan and Joseph would be with him.
Why did Joseph want his family to dwell in the land of Goshen? So they could live comfortably because the Egyptians looked down on anyone who was a shepherd.

Gen. 47   Why didn't Joseph buy the lands belonging to the Priests? The Priests worked for Pharaoh for a salary and their salary was sufficient to pay for their food. They had no need to sell their farms.

Gen. 48   What was God's blessing, as revealed to Joseph by Jacob before he died? "I'm going to make you prosperous and numerous, turn you into a congregation of tribes; and I'll turn this land over to your children coming after you as a permanent inheritance."

Gen. 49   What do you think about the things Israel spoke over each son's life? Open discussion.

Gen. 50   What is your opinion of Joseph? Open discussion.

The Key Points!

What was the Blessing of Abraham? Open discussion. (Gen. 12,15,17)
How does the Blessing of Abraham apply to your life today? Open for discussion.
What can you do to assure the Blessing continues in your life? Open for discussion

THE KEY POINTS!

Tracing the Family of Moses
and
Understanding God's Deliverance of Israel

The Book of
EXODUS

Based on "The Message Bible" by Eugene H. Peterson
Adapted and Written by Joyful Lady Faye Ivey-Jones
Completed: Sunday, February 18, 2007

EXODUS

Tracing the Family of Moses
and
Understanding God's Deliverance of Israel

Jacob (renamed Israel)

Jacob's sons who travel to Egypt: Reuben, Simeon, Levi and Judah;

Issachar, Zebulun, and Benjamin;

Dan, Naphtali, Gad and Asher

A Levites man (Amram) and woman (Jochebed) were parents of Moses and Aaron

Moses together with Zipporah had Gershom and Eliezer

The family of Moses and Aaron (by heads of the tribes)

Sons of Reuben (firstborn of Israel): Hanoch, Pallu, Hezron and Carmi

Sons of Simeon: Jemuel, Jamin, Ohad, Jakin, Zohar, and Saul (son of a Canaanite woman)

Sons of Levi: Gershon, Kohath, and Merari (Levi lived 137 years)

       Sons of Gershon: Libni and Shimei

       Sons of Kohath: Amram (lived 137 years), Izhar, Hebron and Uzziel (Kohath lived 133 years)

                Amram married his aunt Jochebed and together they had Moses and Aaron

                Izhar had Korah, Nepheg and Zicri

                Uzziel Had Mishael, Elzaphan and Sithri

                Aaron married Elisheba daughter of Amminadab and sister of Nahson and had Nadab, Abihi, Eleazar and Ithamar

Sons of Merari: Mahli and Mushi

Sons of Korah: Assir, Elkanah and Abiasaph

Aaron's son Eleazar married one of the daughters of Putiel and had Phinehas.

EXODUS

(Refer to your bible for completion)

These are the names of the Israelites who went to Egypt with Jacob/Israel to join Joseph, each bringing his family members: Reuben, Simeon, Levi, Judah, Issachar, Zebulun, Benjamin, Dan, Naphtali, Gad and Asher; 70 in all generated from Jacob's seed. Joseph, his brothers and all that generation died, but the children of Israel kept on reproducing and they filled the land. Then a new king came into power who did not know Joseph and was alarmed at the number of Israelites living in the land. He demanded that they be treated harshly. The Israelites were then put into work-gangs and put to hard labor under the watchful eyes of gang-foremen. He wanted to get rid of them and continued to plot to kill the boy babies. (Exodus 1)

Why did the king fear the over-population of the Israelites?

What did the king hope to accomplish by treating the Israelites harshly?

How did the king plan to get rid of the Israelites?

Why did the king's plan fail?

A man from the family of Levi married a Levite woman and they had a son. Sensing there was something special about this child the woman hid him until he was 3 months old. No longer able to hide him she then came up with a plan to spare his life. The child was called Moses. Moses grew up and one day went to visit his brothers and saw all the hard labor they were subjected too. His anger over seeing an Egyptian hit one of the Hebrews resulted in his fear for his own life. He escaped to the land of Midian where he met the daughters of the priest. He was invited to their home for a meal. There he settled and married Zipporah and had a son named Gershom. Years later the king of Egypt died and the Israelites cried out to God for relief from their hard labor. God heard them. (Exodus 2)

How did the Levite woman save her baby?

What happened that made Moses fear for his life?

How did Moses meet the daughters of the Midian Priest?

The angel of God appeared to Moses in flames of fire blazing out of the middle of a bush. God instructed Moses to return to Egypt and bring the people of Israel back to the mountain to worship. God assured Moses that He would intervene with miracles that would make the king of Egypt comply. (Exodus 3)

Who was Moses' father-in-law and what was his name?

What was the Mountain of God called?

What were the very first instructions God spoke to Moses? Why?

Moses objected to the responsibility of God's command knowing the people would not believe that God had sent him. God then gave Moses signs of proof to reveal to the people. But Moses still objected because he had little confidence in his ability to speak convincingly. God again assured him that He would be with him. (Exodus 4)

How did God resolve Moses' concerns?

Who was the first to receive the message God had given to Moses?

Who was the Second?

Moses and Aaron went to Pharaoh and spoke God's message. Pharaoh refused to comply and punished the Israelites by giving them extra workload. The people cried out to Moses and accused him of making their life worse than before. Moses asked God why? (Exodus 5)

What was Pharaoh asked to do?

How did Pharaoh punish the Israelites?

Who accused Moses of making things worse for the Israelites?

God told Moses to go to Pharaoh with His message. He was ready to show Pharaoh the hand of God. Moses knowing the people hadn't listened to him because they were so beaten down, didn't think Pharaoh would listen either because he stuttered. God commanded him and Aaron to go. We learn the family tree of Moses. (Exodus 6)

Who were the parents of Aaron and Moses?

Trace the exact family line to Aaron and Moses.

Moses was 80 years old and Aaron was 83 years old when they spoke to Pharaoh. As expected Pharaoh would not listen, so through Moses and Aaron, God performed a miracle. (Exodus 7)

How did Moses first attempt to convince Pharaoh that his God was God?

| |
| |

Moses and Aaron returned again and again and God revealed miracle after miracle, but Pharaoh remained stubborn and refused to let the Israelites go to the wilderness to worship. (Exodus 8)

Even though he remained stubborn, name 2 of the miracles that convinced Pharaoh and his magicians that Moses' God was God?

| |
| |
| |
| |

God reveals more miracles to Pharaoh, but his heart remains hardened. (Exodus 9)

Describe 2 more of the miracles God revealed to Pharaoh.

| |
| |
| |
| |

Pharaoh's servants were fed up and asked Pharaoh how long was he going to allow them to be harassed because Egypt was on its last legs. Pharaoh told them to go, but with conditions. Pharaoh's heart was still hard. (Exodus 10)

Which miracle do you think was the most devastating in this chapter?

| |
| |

Why?

| |
| |

In preparation of their departure, God instructs Moses to have the people to ask their neighbors for silver and gold. Moses and Aaron then again approach Pharaoh with a warning to release the people of Israel. (Exodus 11)

What was God's final warning to Pharaoh?

God told Moses and Aaron, "On the 10th day of the 1st month, each man is to take a healthy, one year old lamb that has been penned until the 14th day and slaughter it at dusk. Then take some of the blood and smear it on the 2 sideposts and the upper doorpost of those houses of the people who will eat it. You are to eat the meat roasted in the fire with bread made without yeast and bitter herbs. Any leftovers you are to burn in the fire. Depending on family size, you may share the lamb with a neighbor's family." God also gave specific instructions on how they were to approach the meal for consumption. (Exodus 12)

What is the name of the "Memorial Day of the Fixed Festival Celebration when God brought Israel out of Egypt?

How was it to be observed?

What do we know that day as today?

Describe the miracle that would be revealed by God during this time?

God told Moses to consecrate the first born from the womb to Him. Moses gave those instructions to the Israelites reminding them to remember the day when God brought them out of Egypt. God led them by a pillar of cloud during the day and by a pillar of fire at night. (Exodus 13)

What day did Moses tell the people to always remember?

In what month does the bible say God brought them out?

Why did God not journey them through the land of the Philistines?

God gave Moses instructions to lead the people in a way that Pharaoh would think they were confused and lost. God planned this to use Pharaoh and his army to put His glory on display. Finally, the Egyptians would realize that He was God. But as planned, Pharaoh led the Egyptian army in chase for the Israelites to force them to return as slaves. As the Egyptian army approached, Moses told the people to watch the hand of God fight the battle for them. God told Moses what to do and the people were delivered. The people now trusted God and his servant Moses. (Exodus 14)

How did God protect the Israelites at Pi Hahiroth?

Together Moses and the Israelites sang a song to God. Miriam the prophetess, who was Aaron's sister, led the woman in singing as they all danced and played tambourines. (Exodus 15)

Divide into groups and develop a tune for the words to their song and name it.

The people moved from Elim into the wilderness of sin between Elim and Sinai. The people complained about the lack of food to eat so God told Moses that He would provide provision for the people and also gave instructions on how they were to consume it. God provided quail in the evenings and bread in the mornings. (Exodus 16)

How was God going to provide the provisions for the Israelites?

What were the instructions they were given concerning the provisions?

What does man-hu mean?

How much provision was to be gathered each day per person?

What was the biggest problem exhibited by the Israelites?

How long did God make provisions for the people?

What were the people instructed to do with the omer?

What is an ephah?

The people continued to complain to Moses and doubted God's provision for them. Moses cried out to God in prayer because he thought the angry people would kill him. God again answered by providing water to drink from a rock.

Moses told Joshua to select men to go out and fight Amalek who had come to fight them. Aaron and Hur gave the necessary support to Moses that helped to win the war. God told Moses to write this as a reminder for Joshua because He would wipe the memory of Amalek off the face of the Earth. Moses built an altar and named it "God My Banner." (Exodus 17)

Where was the rock which provided water?

How were Aaron and Hur helpful in winning the war?

What did Moses say after he built an altar?

Jethro has now heard the reports of all that God had done for Moses and Israel. Zipporah, Gershom and Eliezer, had been sent back to stay with him and they all journeyed to visit Moses in the wilderness. After hearing the stories from Moses, Jethro offered up a Whole Burnt Offering and sacrifices to God. Jethro could see that Moses grew tired from judging the people and teaching them God's laws and instructions from morning until night. He made a suggestion that would help Moses. (Exodus 18)

Describe Jethro's suggestive plan to help Moses.

The Israelites entered the Wilderness of Sinai by route of Rephidim 3 months after leaving Egypt. God told Moses what to tell the House of Jacob. The people unanimously agreed to do what God said and Moses told God of their response. God's instruction for the people was to scrub their clothes and prepare themselves by the 3rd day when He would make His presence known to them. God instructed Moses to set boundaries for the people because no one was to touch even the edge of the mountain in which He would appear. When Moses went up to speak with God, God sent him back down to remind the people not to touch the mountain. God asked for Aaron. (Exodus 19)

What was God going to do so that the people would trust Moses?

Moses told the people not to be afraid because God has come to test you and instill a deep and reverent awe within you so that you won't sin. But the people were afraid and kept their distance sending Moses to speak with God. (Exodus 20)

What was most significant about this message God gave the people?

God gave further instructions to Moses for the people concerning the rights and penalties for the injury and/or treatment of slaves, animals and family members. He gave the penalty for reckless behaviors and acts of intentional and unintentional murder. (Exodus 21 / 22)

How do you think these types of laws would affect today's society?

God's instructions on penalty for the resolution of behaviors of the people continues and He gives a reminder of the celebration of the Festival of Unraised Bread. (Exodus 23)

Why would God slowly remove the Hittites from the land and not all at once?

God allowed Moses to climb the mountain to worship Him and allowed others to come along. The next morning Moses built an altar at the foot of the mountain, directed the young men to make a Whole Burnt Offering and then read to them the Book of the Covenant. The people agreed to do everything that God had said. God told Moses to climb higher on the mountain and there He would give Moses the tablets of stone, the teachings and commandments written to instruct the people. (Exodus 24)

Who went along with Moses when he climbed the mountain to worship?

How long was Moses on the mountain?

God said to Moses: "Tell the Israelites that they are to set aside offerings for me. Receive the offerings from everyone who is willing to give." God further described the offerings that He wanted Moses to receive. (Exodus 25-28)

Divide into groups and construct a collage of the Offerings.
Draw a picture of the Chest.
Draw a picture of the Table.
Construct 1 lamp according to God's instructions
Collectively, decide and construct a replica of the Dwelling
Collectively, decide and construct a replica of the Altar.
Divide into groups and design the Vestment.
Divide into groups and design the Ephod.
Divide into groups and design the Breastpiece.
Divide into groups and design the Robe.
Divide into groups and design the Turban, Tunic, and Underwear.

This chapter describes the manner of consecrating the priests. (Exodus 29)

Who were the men to be consecrated as priests?

| |
| |

This chapter describes the construction of the Altar of Incense, the giving of the "Atonement Tax", the purpose of the "Washbasin", the mixing of the "Holy Anointing Oil and the "Holy Incense". (Exodus 30)

The men will build the "Altar of Incense"
(All who are 21years and over be prepared to give "Atonement Tax" in Sunday's offering.)
The women will seek and provide the "Washbasin".
The men will mix the "Holy Anointing Oil".
The women will make the "Holy Incense".

God spoke to Moses as to remind the people that above, all to keep His Sabbath. The Sabbath is the sign between God and His people, generation after generation, to keep the knowledge alive that God is our God who makes us holy. (Exodus 31)

When God finished talking to Moses on Mount Sinai, what did He give to him?

| |
| |

The people grew impatient waiting for Moses to descend the mountain and asked Aaron to make them gods to lead them. Aaron told them to bring their gold jewelry and he made a golden calf. Aaron then built an altar before the calf and announced "Tomorrow is a feast day to God." The people prayed then began to eat and drink and soon there was a wild party. God told Moses to go down to the people who had fallen to pieces. God was angry because they were hard-headed and He wanted to incinerate them. Moses pleaded with God to remember His word for Abraham, Isaac and Israel. God decided not to do evil to the people. Moses returned to the people as they were partying and his anger flared. He smashed the tablets given to him by God. He destroyed the calf and punished the people. Moses called for all those who were on God's side to come to him. For all the others, he ordered the Levities to kill 3,000 that day. Moses then went back to God hoping to clear the people of their sins. God sent a plague on the people because of the calf they and Aaron had made. (Exodus 32)

How did Moses punish the people?

| |
| |

Who were the people God said He would erase from the Book?

```
┌─────────────────────────────────────────────────────────────┐
│                                                             │
├─────────────────────────────────────────────────────────────┤
│                                                             │
└─────────────────────────────────────────────────────────────┘
```

God told Moses to go and take the people to the land that He had promised to give to the descendants of Abraham, Isaac and Jacob. God would not go with them in person but was going to send an angel ahead and drive out the Canaanites, Amorites, Hittites, Perizzites, Hivites, and Jebusites. The people knew God was angry with Israel. Whenever Moses entered the Tent of Meeting, the people stood at attention as he entered. The Pillar of Cloud descended to the entrance of the Tent of Meeting and as God spoke with Moses each man bowed down at the entrance of his own tent to worship. Moses asked God to lead the way. God agreed but told Moses he could not see His face. Moses would only see God's back. (Exodus 33)

Why didn't God want to go with the people as they journeyed to the Promised Land?

```
┌─────────────────────────────────────────────────────────────┐
│                                                             │
├─────────────────────────────────────────────────────────────┤
│                                                             │
└─────────────────────────────────────────────────────────────┘
```

God instructed Moses to cut out 2 tablets of stone just like the original one he smashed and to engrave the same words that had been on the original tablets. Moses had to meet God at the top of Mount Sinai and no other person or animal was to come on the mountain. God made a covenant with Moses and instructed him to remain vigilant as he entered the Promise Land and not to become friendly with the inhabitants there. They were to remember the Feast of Unraised Bread and abide by God's instructions regarding it. Moses didn't eat or drink anything in the 40 days and nights he was with God on Mount Sinai. He wrote on the tablets the words of the covenant. When Moses descended the mountain he told the people all that God had told him and they were afraid of him. (Exodus 34)

What did the people have to do in order to not worry about their land?

```
┌─────────────────────────────────────────────────────────────┐
│                                                             │
├─────────────────────────────────────────────────────────────┤
│                                                             │
└─────────────────────────────────────────────────────────────┘
```

Why were the people afraid of Moses when he descended the mountain?

```
┌─────────────────────────────────────────────────────────────┐
│                                                             │
├─────────────────────────────────────────────────────────────┤
│                                                             │
└─────────────────────────────────────────────────────────────┘
```

Moses spoke to the people and told them how God wanted them to work 6 days only and to rest on the 7th day as well as the penalty for disobedience. He also told them what God said regarding offerings and the works they were to do. Those who had a heart and mind to, went home and returned with their freewill offerings. God selected Bezalel son of Uri, son of Hur of the tribe of Judah, and Oholiab son of Ahisamach, of the tribe of Dan, filled them with the Spirit of God and with skill, ability and know-how for design and work in gold, silver, bronze etc. They could design and make anything. (Exodus 35)

What types of things did the people bring to build the Tent of Meeting?

What did the leaders bring?

Bezalel and Oholiab along with all those skillful willing workers who God had given the ability to work with their hands began to work, as God commanded making everything involved in the worship of the Sanctuary. The people kept bringing their offerings morning after morning until there was much more than enough, so Moses sent out orders throughout the camp and ordered the people to stop bringing offerings! (Exodus 36)

Who did Moses call to begin construction of the Sanctuary besides Bezalel and Ohliab?

The construction of the Sanctuary is underway (Exodus 37)

What was the size of the finished Chest?

The construction of the Sanctuary is still underway. (Exodus 38)

How much gold was used to construct the Sanctuary?

How much silver was used to construct the Sanctuary?

What is today's equivalent of a half-shekel?

How much bronze was used to construct the Sanctuary?

The construction of the Sanctuary is nearing completion (Exodus 39)

Describe the design and the place where you will find the name of the sons of Israel and give the reason it is there.

Describe the colors of the stones mounted on 4 rows of the breast-piece.

God told Moses to set up The Dwelling of the Tent of Meeting. Moses put everything in its proper place and anointed Aaron and his sons. He consecrated them to serve as priests just as God commanded him. The Cloud of God covered the Tent of Meeting and the Glory of God filled The Dwelling during the day and the fire was in it at night visible to all the Israelites in all their travels. (Exodus 40)

Why couldn't Moses enter the Tent of Meeting?

Draw a replica of the "The Dwelling of the Tent of Meeting."

THE KEY POINTS!

EXODUS
Bible Review Quiz

EXODUS 1   Why did the king fear the over-population of the Israelites?

What did the king hope to accomplish by treating the Israelites harshly?

How did the king plan to get rid of the Israelites?

Why did the king's plan fail?

EXODUS 2   How did the Levite woman save her baby?

What happened that made Moses fear for his life?

How did Moses meet the daughters of the Midian Priest?

EXODUS 3   Who was Moses' father-in-law and what was his name?

What was the Mountain of God called?

What were the very first instructions God spoke to Moses? Why?

Why?

EXODUS 4   How did God resolve Moses' concerns?

Who was the first to receive the message God had given to Moses?

Who was the Second?

EXODUS 5   What was Pharaoh asked to do?

How did Pharaoh punish the Israelites?

Who accused Moses of making things worse for the Israelites?

_____

EXODUS 6   Who were the parents of Aaron and Moses?

_____

Trace the exact family line to Aaron and Moses.

EXODUS 7   How did Moses first attempt to convince Pharaoh that his God was God?

EXODUS 8   Even though he remained stubborn, name 2 of the miracles that convinced Pharaoh and his magicians that Moses' God was God?

EXODUS 9   Describe 2 more of the miracles God revealed to Pharaoh.

EXODUS 10   Which miracle do you think was the most devastating in this chapter?

Why?

_____
_____

EXODUS 11   What was God's final warning to Pharaoh?

_____
_____

EXODUS 12   What is the name of the memorial day of fixed, festival celebration when God brought Israel out of Egypt?

_____
_____

How was it to be observed?

_____
_____

What do we know that day as today?

_____
_____

Describe the miracle that would be revealed by God during this time?

_____
_____

EXODUS 13   What day did Moses tell the people to always remember?

_____

In what month does the bible say God brought them out?

_____

Why did God not journey them through the land of the Philistines?

_____
_____
_____
_____

EXODUS 14   How did God protect the Israelites at Pi Hahiroth?

| |
| |

EXODUS 15   Divide into groups and develop a tune for the words to their song and name it.

| |

EXODUS 16   How was God going to provide the provisions for the Israelites?

| |
| |
| |
| |

What were the instructions they were given concerning the provisions?

| |
| |
| |
| |

What does man-hu mean?

| |
| |

How much provision was to be gathered each day per person?

| |
| |

What was the biggest problem exhibited by the Israelites?

| |
| |
| |
| |

How long did God make provisions for the people?

What were the people instructed to do with the omer?

What is an ephah?

EXODUS 17   Where was the rock which provided water?

How were Aaron and Hur helpful in winning the war?

What did Moses say after he built an altar?

EXODUS 18   Describe Jethro's suggestive plan to help Moses.

EXODUS 19   What was God going to do so that the people would trust Moses?

EXODUS 20   What was most significant about this message God gave the people?

EXODUS 21   How do you think these types of laws would affect today's society?

EXODUS 22   How do you think these types of laws would affect today's society?

EXODUS 23   Why would God slowly remove the Hittites from the land and not all at once?

EXODUS 24   Who went along with Moses when he climbed the mountain to worship?

How long was Moses on the mountain?

EXODUS 25   Divide into groups and construct a collage of the Offerings.
Draw a picture of the Chest.
Draw a picture of the Table.
Construct 1 lamp according to God's instructions

EXODUS 26   Collectively, decide and construct a replica of the Dwelling.

EXODUS 27   Collectively, decide and construct a replica of the Altar.

EXODUS 28   Divide into groups and design the Vestment.
Divide into groups and design the Ephod.
Divide into groups and design the Breastpiece.
Divide into groups and design the Robe.
Divide into groups and design the Turban, Tunic, and Underwear.

EXODUS 29   Who were the men to be consecrated as priests?

| |
| |

EXODUS 30   The men will build the "Altar of Incense"
(All who are 21 years and over be prepared to give "Atonement Tax"
in Sunday's offering.)
The women will seek and provide the "Washbasin".
The men will mix the "Holy Anointing Oil".
The women will make the "Holy Incense".

EXODUS 31   When God finished talking to Moses on Mount Sinai, what did He
give to him?

| |
| |

EXODUS 32   How did Moses punish the people?

| |
| |
| |
| |

Who were the people God said He would erase from the Book?

| |
| |

EXODUS 33   Why didn't God want to go with the people as they journeyed to the Promised Land?

| |
| |

EXODUS 34   What did the people have to do in order to not worry about their land?

| |
| |

Why were the people afraid of Moses when he descended the mountain?

| |
| |

EXODUS 35   What types of things did the people bring to build the Tent of Meeting?

| |

What did the leaders bring?

| |

EXODUS 36   Who did Moses call to begin construction of the Sanctuary besides Bezalel and Ohliab?

| |

EXODUS 37   What was the size of the finished Chest?

| |

EXODUS 38   How much gold was used to construct the Sanctuary?

| |

How much silver was used to construct the Sanctuary?

| |

What is today's equivalent of a half-shekel?

How much bronze was used to construct the Sanctuary?

EXODUS 39   Describe the design and the place where you will find the name of the sons of Israel; and give the reason it is there.

Describe the colors of the stones mounted on 4 rows of the breastpiece.

EXODUS 40   Why couldn't Moses enter the Tent of Meeting?

Draw a replica of the "The Dwelling of the Tent of Meeting."

The Key Points!

What led up to Israel's cries to God for the deliverance of Israel?

Why was Moses unable to accomplish God's plan of deliverance immediately?

What are the similarities between the deliverance of Israel and our deliverance today?

EXODUS-1
<u>The Key Points!</u>

EXODUS

Bible Review Quiz—Answer Sheet

EXODUS 1   Why did the king fear the over-population of the Israelites?
He thought they would join forces with the enemy in war against Egypt.
What did the king hope to accomplish by treating the Israelites harshly? He hoped that they would be so over-worked they would stop reproducing children.
How did the king plan to get rid of the Israelites? He ordered the midwives to kill all boy babies at the time of birth.
Why did the king's plan fail? The midwives respected God too much to kill the babies. They spared their lives and told the king that the Hebrew women gave birth before they could arrive.

EXODUS 2   How did the Levite woman save her baby? She made a basket to put him in and floated him on the Nile River for Pharaoh's daughter to find.
What happened that made Moses fear for his life? Word had gotten out that he had killed an Egyptian.
How did Moses meet the daughters of the Midian Priest? He came to the rescue of the daughters when a bunch of shepherds chased them off from watering their sheep.

EXODUS 3   Who was Moses' father-in-law and what was his name? Jethro, the priest of Midian.
What was the Mountain of God called? Horab
What were the very first instructions God spoke to Moses? Why? "Don't come any closer; remove your sandals from your feet." Because he was standing on holy ground.

EXODUS 4   How did God resolve Moses' concerns? He first showed Moses the signs that he could use to make the people believe. Then He told Moses that Aaron would go with him to speak for him.
Who was the first to receive the message God had given to Moses? The Second? Aaron was the 1st, and all the leaders of Israel were the 2nd.

1

EXODUS-2

EXODUS 5   What was Pharaoh asked to do? To let the Hebrews go to the wilderness to worship God.

How did Pharaoh punish the Israelites? He ordered that they no longer be given straw to make bricks. They now had to gather their own straw and still meet their quota of daily bricks.

Who accused Moses of making things worse for the Israelites? The Israelites' foremen.

EXODUS 6   Who were the parents of Aaron and Moses? Amram and Jochebed

Trace the exact family line to Aaron and Moses. Noah had Shem, after many generations came Nahor who had Terah, Terah had Abraham, Abraham had Issac, Issac had Jacob, Jacob (now Israel) had Levi the priest, Levi had Kohath, Kohath had Amram, and Amram had Aaron and Moses.

EXODUS 7   How did Moses first attempt to convince Pharaoh that his God was God? Aaron threw down Moses' staff and God turned it into a snake.

EXODUS 8   Even though Paraoh remained stubborn, name 2 of the miracles that convinced Pharaoh and his magicians that Moses' God was God? 1. The dust of the earth being turned into gnats: 2. The frogs that covered the land; 3. The release of the swarm of flies that covered only the Egyptians but not the Israelites.

EXODUS 9   Describe 2 more of the miracles God revealed to Pharaoh. 1. God caused all the animals in the fields that belonged to the Egyptians to die of a severe disease; 2. God told Moses to throw fistfuls of soot from a furnace into the air and He caused it to become a film of dust and cause sores and boils on the people and animals throughout Egypt. 3. God told Moses to stretch his hands to the skies and God sent a fierce hail storm on all the animals and workers exposed out in the field. People, animals, crops and trees were destroyed, except for Goshen.

EXODUS 10   Which miracle do you think was the most devastating in this chapter? Why? Open discussion. 1. The locusts covering and devouring the land or; 2. Complete darkness covering the land for 3 days.

EXODUS 11   What was God's final warning to Pharaoh? That every firstborn child in Egypt would die including animals.

EXODUS-3

EXODUS 12   What is the name of the memorial day of fixed festival celebration when God brought Israel out of Egypt? The Festival of Unraised Bread
How was it to be observed? They had to remove all yeast from their houses and were to eat matzoth from the evening on the 14th day until the evening of the 21st day in the 1st month, a total of 7 days to avoid being cut off from the community of Israel. Also the 1st and 7th days were set aside as holy days where they could do no work except prepare meals.
What do we know that day as today? Passover.
Describe the miracle that would be revealed by God during this time? God would go through the land of Egypt and strike down every firstborn in the land and bring judgment on all the gods of Egypt. The blood would serve as a sign on the houses where the Israelites live and God would pass over causing no disaster there.

EXODUS 13   What day did Moses tell the people to always remember? The day when they came out of Egypt from a house of slavery.
In what month does the bible say God brought them out? The spring month of Abib (April)
Why did God not journey them through the land of the Philistines? God thought if they encountered war they would return to Egypt.

EXODUS 14   How did God protect the Israelites at Pi Hahiroth? The angel of God that had been leading the camp of Israel now shifted and got behind them positioning the Pillar of Cloud between the Israelites and the Egyptians.

EXODUS 15   Divide into groups and develop a tune for the words to their song and name it.

EXODUS 16   How was God going to provide the provisions for the Israelites?
He was going to rain down bread from the skies.
What were the instructions they were given concerning the provisions? They were to gather only enough for that day but on the 6th day they were to gather and prepare enough for 2 days.
What does man-hu mean? (What is it?)
How much provision was to be gathered each day per person? 2 quarts.
What was the biggest problem exhibited by the Israelites?
They were disobedient.
How long did God make provisions for the people? 40 years.

EXODUS-4

What were the people instructed to do with the omer? Keep it for future generation so they can see the bread that God fed the people in the wilderness after He brought them out of Egypt.
What is an ephah? It is an instrument of measure equivalent to .65 Bushel or 20.8 quarts.

EXODUS 17   Where was the rock which provided water? Horeb
How were Aaron and Hur helpful in winning the war? They each supported the hands of Moses that held up the staff.
What did Moses say after he built an altar? Salute God's rule! God at war with Amalek always and forever!

EXODUS 18   Describe Jethro's suggestive plan to help Moses. Moses should select competent men who fear God, who had integrity and were incorruptible to be over groups of men that could assist with the routine cases for judging. Therefore Moses could get rest because he would get only the hard cases.

EXODUS 19   What was God going to do so that the people would trust Moses? Come to Moses in a thick cloud so the people could listen in when He spoke.

EXODUS 20   What was most significant about this message God gave the people? This message revealed the laws or commandments by which God expects us to live even until today!

EXODUS 21   How do you think these types of laws would affect today's society? Open discussion.

EXODUS 22   How do you think these types of laws would affect today's society? Open discussion.

EXODUS 23   Why would God slowly remove the Hittites from the land and not remove them all at once? So that the land would not grow up in weeds and the animals wouldn't take over. God used them to till the land until Israel could get their crops going.

EXODUS 24   Who went along with Moses when he climbed the mountain to worship? Aaron, Nadab, Abihu and 70 of the elders of Israel.
How long was Moses on the mountain? 40 days and 40 nights

EXODUS-5

EXODUS 25   Divide into groups and construct a collage of the Offerings.
Draw a picture of the Chest.
Draw a picture of the Table.
Construct 1 lamp according to God's instructions

EXODUS 26   Collectively, decide and construct a replica of the Dwelling.

EXODUS 27   Collectively, decide and construct a replica of the Altar.

EXODUS 28   Divide into groups and design the Vestment.
Divide into groups and design the Ephod.
Divide into groups and design the Breastpiece.
Divide into groups and design the Robe.
Divide into groups and design the Turban, Tunic, and Underwear.

EXODUS 29   Who were the men to be consecrated as priests? Aaron and all his descendent sons.

EXODUS 30   The men will build the "Altar of Incense"
(All who are 21years and over be prepared to give "Atonement Tax" in Sunday's offering.)
The women will seek and provide the "Washbasin".
The men will mix the "Holy Anointing Oil".
The women will make the "Holy Incense".

EXODUS 31   When God finished talking to Moses on Mount Sinai, what did He give to him? 2 tablets of Testimony, slabs of stone, written with the finger of God.

EXODUS 32   How did Moses punish the people? He melted the calf, pulverized it to powder then scattered it on the water and made the Israelites drink it. Who were the people God said He would erase from the Book? Only those people who sin against Him.

EXODUS 33   Why didn't God want to go with the people as they journeyed to the Promised Land? God said they were such a stubborn, hard-headed people and He would destroy them on the journey.

EXODUS 34   What did the people have to do in order to not worry about their land? They had to appear before the Master, the God of Israel, 3 times a year. Why were the people afraid of Moses when he descended the mountain? Because his face glowed.

EXODUS-6

EXODUS 35   What types of things did the people bring to build the Tent of Meeting? Broaches, earrings, rings, necklaces all of Gold. Blue, purple and scarlet fabrics, fine linen, goats' hair, tanned leather and dolphin skins. Silver or bronze, acacia wood.
What did the leaders bring? Onyx and other precious stones, spices, olive oil and incense.

EXODUS 36   Who did Moses call to begin construction of the Sanctuary besides Bezalel and Ohliab? Everyone whom God had given the skill and know-how for making everything involved in the worship of the Sanctuary.

EXODUS 37   What was the size of the finished Chest? Approximately, 3 ¾ feet long and 2 ¼ feet wide.

EXODUS 38   How much gold was used to construct the Sanctuary? 1,900 pounds
How much silver was used to construct the Sanctuary? 6,437 pounds
What is today's equivalent of a half-shekel? 1/5 ounce
How much bronze was used to construct the Sanctuary? 4,522 pounds

EXODUS 39   Describe the design and the place where you will find the name of the sons of Israel; and give the reason it is there. Their names were engraved on onyx stones in a setting of filigreed gold and fastened on the shoulder pieces of the Ephod as memorial stones for the Israelites. Describe the colors of the stones mounted on 4 rows of the breast piece. Color samples must be submitted.
First Row: carnelian, topaz, emerald
Second Row: ruby, sapphire, crystal
Third Row: jacinth, agate, amethyst
Fourth Row: beryl, onyx, jasper

EXODUS 40   Why couldn't Moses enter the Tent of Meeting? Because the Cloud of God was upon it and the Glory of God filled The Dwelling.

The Key Points!

What led up to Israel's cries to God for the deliverance of Israel? Open discussion. (Exodus 1)

Why was Moses unable to accomplish God's plan of deliverance immediately? Open discussion.

What are the similarities between the deliverance of Israel and our deliverance today? Open discussion.

About the Author

Faye Ivey-Jones, known as "Joyful Lady" enjoys the journey of her life! She grew up as a very active child spending a large part of her life at her neighborhood church participating in Sunday school, playing piano, the youth choir, girl scouts and serving as color guard captain in the neighborhood Riversiders Drum and Bugle Corp., and Warriors Drum and Bugle Corp., as a member of the trick-rifle squad. She enjoyed playing handball, bike riding, roller-skating and ice-skating. She studied nursing but quickly found this lifestyle too confining and preferred surrounding herself with a more joyful, relaxed atmosphere. She enjoyed the union of marriage for nineteen years before the death of her husband, and raised three children and numerous Godchildren. She is most proud of her children who are all educated, independent, upstanding citizens with the youngest recently graduating with a Masters in Social Work. She graduated and worked at the Nassau Community College. She loves teaching children which is evidenced by her fifteen-year experience as Owner/Director/Teacher of "Progressive Movement Dance Studio." She was also a teacher's assistance at Harry Daniels Primary Center in the Roosevelt School District, choreographer for Sisters' Circle Gospel Community Theatre and presently Director of the Children's Ministry at her church. She also presently works full-time servicing clients at the Dept. of Social Services. She rededicated her life to Christ in 1995 and since lives as a devout Christian. She is mindful and obedient to walk in the Call on her life. Her Call includes writing *"The Key Points!"* series with the goal of ushering souls into the Kingdom by reaching youths and adults alike who are drawn to God but seek the ease of a helping hand in finding their way. Her love for God, her family and all His people continues!